A Dozen Dramatic

in

Cornwall

James Clancy

and

Simone Stanbrook-Byrne

CULM VALLEY PUBLISHING

Published by

Culm Valley Publishing Ltd
Culmcott House
Mill Street, Uffculme
Cullompton, Devon
EX15 3AT, UK
Tel: +44(0)1884 849085
Fax: +44(0)1884 840251
E-mail: info@culmvalleypublishing.co.uk
Website: www.culmvalleypublishing.co.uk

While every effort has been made to ensure the accuracy of the information contained in
this book, the publisher and authors accept no liability for incorrect details or changes
regarding public footpaths, rights of way and tourist information. Neither Culm Valley
Publishing Ltd nor the authors shall be liable for any damages whatsoever arising in any
way from the use of or inability to use this book, or any material contained within it, or
from any action or decision taken as a result of using this book. Follow the country code.

First published 2011

ISBN 978-1-907942-03-7 paperback

British Library Cataloguing-in-Publication Data
A catalogue record for this book is available from the British Library

Typeset by Culm Valley Publishing Ltd
Printed and bound by T.J. International Ltd, Padstow, Cornwall

Front cover image: Lion Rock, near Kynance Cove (Walk 4)
Back cover image: Coastline at Portnadler Bay (Walk 9)

Contents

Introduction

Writing this walking guide has been great fun. The authors have enjoyed the 'research' very much – the struggle to attain the highest points, route-finding on elusive paths, fabulous views, pubs with open fires or sunny gardens – and the reward of ending the day where we intended.

By virtue of their nature 'dramatic walks' can involve challenging terrain so whenever you embark on a walk, common sense must prevail: be properly shod and take care where you put your feet, be prepared for any kind of weather, take food and first aid supplies with you and make sure someone knows where you're going. Mobile phones are often useless in the middle of nowhere.

We also feel it's **imperative** that you take the **correct OS map** with you plus a **compass**, and are conversant with their use. Our sketch maps are precisely that – sketches – and are for rough guidance only and are not to scale.

You know you've had a good day's walking when you get home safely at the end of it and haven't been overtaken by the drama.

Useful websites:
A useful site which gives tips for moorland treks is: www.tourbytor.co.uk/equip_walk.php

Follow the countryside code:
www.naturalengland.org.uk/ourwork/enjoying/countrysidecode/default.aspx

Our grateful thanks to:
Rosemary and Paul Clancy for fab food and accommodation;
Brian and Jenny Willan for a lovely office and cherry tarts;
Norman Govier for mine history snippets
Nic and Ella, Tony and William

Disclaimer

Points that should be borne in mind on any route – dramatic or not:

Public footpaths can be legally re-routed from the path shown on the map. In such cases they are usually clearly signposted. Where this has happened before the time of writing it has been noted in the text.

Most public footpaths are on private land. Please respect this.

Don't be surprised to find livestock grazing on public footpaths – and treat all animals with caution and respect.

If a field is planted with crops across a footpath, provision is usually made around the edge of the field.

Landmarks can change: trees and hedges may disappear; streams can dry up in warm weather; stiles turn into gates and vice versa; fences appear where previously there was no boundary. Even views are different as the seasons progress. In such cases a modicum of common sense must be exercised – in conjunction with the map.

Public footpaths are at times blocked by barbed wire etc. Should this render the route impassable find the shortest detour around that section.

Please leave gates as you find them and if you have to climb them do so at the hinge end where it's stronger.

Exercise caution on wet stiles – they can be extremely slippery.

Take all your rubbish with you, don't damage anything during the walk and don't pick plants.

Keep your dogs under proper control.

We hope that you enjoy these walks without mishap, but urge you to exercise common sense at all times! Neither the authors nor Culm Valley Publishing Ltd accepts responsibility for any misadventure which may occur during, or arise from, these walks and suggested routes.

Walk Locations

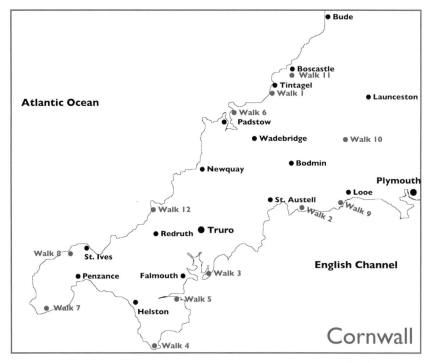

Walk 1   Trebarwith Strand & Tintagel
Walk 2   Bodinnick & the Fowey Estuary
Walk 3   St. Anthony Head
Walk 4   Lizard & Kynance Cove
Walk 5   Helford River & Frenchman's Creek
Walk 6   Polzeath
Walk 7   Treen & Porthcurno
Walk 8   Zennor
Walk 9   Talland Bay & Polperro
Walk 10 Bodmin Moor & the Cheesewring
Walk 11 Boscastle & Rocky Valley
Walk 12 Chapel Porth & Trevaunance Cove

Meeting of ways (Walk 7)

Walk 1
Trebarwith Strand & Tintagel

Dramatic coastal scenery combined with what is probably a world-famous legend combine to make this a really classic walk. The abundant bird and plant life is exceptionally good, and the inland stretch of field walking has some of the most creative stile arrangements we have come across! There are the expected ascents and descents which one would expect to find in this kind of terrain.

Map: OS Explorer 111, Bude, Boscastle & Tintagel 1:25 000
Start point: Trebarwith Strand. Postcode: PL34 0HB. Grid ref: SX052864
Directions to start: Trebarwith Strand is south of Tintagel, off the B3263
Parking: There are a couple of car parks at Trebarwith Strand, both are easily accessible
Distance: 6½ miles / 10.5km
Refreshments: Lewis's, Tintagel: 01840 770427; Strand Café, Trebarwith Strand: 01840 779482; The Port William, Trebarwith Strand: 01840 770230; Tintagel Castle Beach Café: 01840 779188
Toilets: These are well-signed at Trebarwith Strand, near Tintagel Castle Beach Café and in Tintagel town
Nearby places to stay: This area is awash with a great variety of holiday accommodation such as The Avalon Guest House, Tintagel: 01840 77016. Another particularly nice one in Tintagel is Lewis's: 01840 770427
Nearby places of interest: The Old Post Office, Tintagel (NT): 01840 770024; Tintagel Castle: 01840 770328
Possible birds include: Blackbird, blue tit, buzzard, carrion crow, chiffchaff, dipper, fulmar, great tit, gulls of various hues, house sparrow, jackdaw, peregrine, rook, skylark, wheatear, wren
Authors' tip: If the weather is conducive allow time to sit outside The Port William at Trebarwith Strand when the tide is high. You won't get a more majestic background for a refreshment stop

When you arrive in Trebarwith Strand your first view of the sea is dominated by the mighty Gull Rock out in the bay. Walk down the lane towards it and you will find, on your right, the coast path to Tintagel, 2¼ miles away. Take this, ascending up onto the cliffs. At the top the views back down to the beach are excellent and, at high tide, the pounding waves impressive.

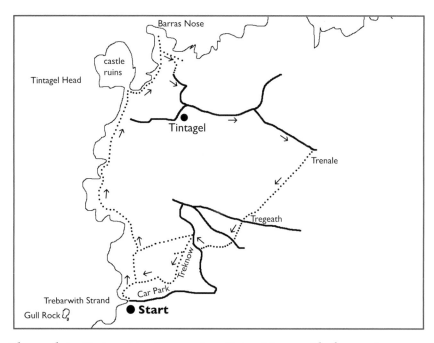

The path to Tintagel is clear and well-trodden, with the sea to your left and stunning views all along this coastline. Ahead you can see Tintagel Church. When you find options to take paths inland ignore them and keep to the coast. Occasionally there are also options to detour onto headlands for vaster views – take these if you wish but be cautious on the edges, as your route follows the coast path all the way to Tintagel Castle and an untimely plummet would delay your arrival. This stretch of walking is beautiful but can also be wild. In spring and early summer the cliffs are a cascade of pink thrift and keep an eye open for the silken 'tents' of lackey moth caterpillars in the hawthorn trees.

The grassy cliff path eventually reaches a surfaced crossing path which leads to the youth hostel, the church is still ahead of you. Visiting the church is an option, alternatively keep to the path following the coastline with the edifice of Camelot Castle Hotel looming ahead of you. Look down to the left below the hotel where you will see the island site of a ruined castle, one of the many alleged to have been associated with the legendary King Arthur. Whatever the truth behind the legend, the setting is spectacular. Follow the path as it goes past the entrance to the castle (English Heritage), visiting it if you wish, then descend to meet the lane below, where you will find various facilities. Here partake of a 'comfort break' before continuing on up the coast path – the way is clearly signed at the far end of Tintagel Castle Beach Café.

Continue on the coast path away from the castle ruins. Barras Nose is the headland to your left with its massive cave. When you reach a fork in the path it's worth taking the left option to explore the headland and enjoy the coastal views in each direction. After this return to the coast path, the hotel still looms above you to the right.

At the next waymarker post take the option to head inland towards Tintagel, leaving the coast path. This leads you up to the hotel's main gates. From here walk along the road away from the hotel.

Sea cave, Barras Nose

Looking back towards Tintagel Castle

At the end of the road follow it as it bends right and continue all the way through the town – an interesting place to visit in its own right with lots of attractions. Pass the National Trust's Old Post Office on your right and later the modern-day equivalent. Keep on through the town until near the end of the houses you find Trenale Lane on your right. Take this as far as the hamlet of Trenale.

As you enter the hamlet look out for a track on the right. Take this and within a few metres take a footpath over a stile on the right signposted for Tregeath. Here begins a series of fields and intricate stile arrangements worthy of a cross-country event. Cross the first stile and turn left, keeping the hedge on your left. Continue beyond the next stile through a second field, the hedge still to your left.

The third stile is a double, cross this and bear diagonally right through the field to the far boundary where you will find a stone-stepped stile to negotiate. After this bear diagonally right again and this line brings you to another double, wood followed by stone. Not particularly dog-friendly this one. Beyond here bear diagonally right again across the next field to the next stile. After this one keep straight ahead with the boundary on your left and at the end of this field you will find a stile-footbridge-stile arrangement. After this continue ahead with the boundary still to your left. This leads to a triple stile beyond which go diagonally right to the far corner of the field. Here you find the best of all. Stone steps lead up to a broad, grassy bank. Walk across and descend steps on the other side.

Walk ahead now through the barnyard of Tregeath Farm to reach a lane. Directly across the lane pick up another footpath and head straight across the field to the next stile. After this bear right to another stile leading onto the road – this is the B3263 so watch out for traffic. Immediately opposite is another stile with a footpath sign. Bear right across the field in the direction indicated to the far

Trebarwith Strand and Gull Rock

Tintagel Castle

The ruins you see before you are 13thC, the castle being built by the Earl of Cornwall in 1233. However, the site has a much older history and a monastery once existed here. Pottery and glass fragments dating from the 5thC to 7thC have been found during excavation plus a piece of fifteen hundred year old Latin-inscribed slate. The area of Tintagel was once a Roman settlement and subsequently, in the Dark Ages, became a trading post for Celtic kings during an era when the country was divided into kingdoms, each governed by its own ruler. The association with King Arthur is open to discussion. The warlord, Owain Ddantgwyn, who has been shown by some sources to be the most likely candidate, predated the castle by many centuries although he may have had a connection with the site during the 6thC. He commanded the Britons at this time and went by the epithet 'The Bear'. The name 'Arthur' means 'bear'.

boundary where you will find another stile – don't go through one of the many gaps as you will be off the path. The stile was a bit broken down at the time of writing and was followed by a picket gate, after which turn immediately right to follow the right hand boundary to a farm gate by some sheds. Go through the gate and past the sheds to a stile on the left. Cross this then continue with the fence on your right, houses are ahead of you. This line leads to another stile after which continue to yet another which then leads onto a narrow path. Reach the lane at Treknow and turn right.

In about 100m you find a track on the left between the Atlantic View Hotel and a grassy triangle with a bench. Go left here and immediately left again to follow a broad track, soon passing the Bluff Centre on the left. This leads you into a seriously beautiful view over Trebarwith Strand and Gull Rock. The path drops to join the coast path along which you turn left to retrace your steps to your starting point. A superb finish.

Bodinnick & the Fowey Estuary

This very attractive route is easy and clear to follow although some paths might be muddy after wet weather. There are some short ascents but nothing too onerous. The 'there and back again' section at the far end is a little gem. The wooded path above Pont Pill is awash with wild flowers in spring and swans breed in the creek so there is a good chance of seeing their delightful cygnets.

Map: OS Explorer 107, St Austell & Liskeard 1:25 000	
Start point: Bodinnick. Postcode: PL23 1LX. Grid ref: SX131522	
Directions to start: Bodinnick can be accessed to the south west off the B3359	
Parking: Free car park on the road towards the ferry	
Distance: 3 miles / 4.8km	
Refreshments: The Old Ferry Inn, Bodinnick: 01726 870237	
Toilets: None en route	
Nearby places to stay: The Old Ferry Inn, Bodinnick: 01726 870237; The Dwelling House, Fowey: 01726 833662	
Nearby places of interest: The town of Fowey across the estuary, which can be accessed via ferry from Bodinnick; Eden Project, Bodelva: 01726 811911	
Possible birds include: Blackbird, buzzard, carrion crow, chaffinch, chiffchaff, dunnock, goldfinch, grey wagtail, gulls of various hues, jackdaw, jay, mallard, mute swan, pheasant, robin, song thrush, skylark, woodpigeon, yellowhammer	
Authors' tip: A short drive to the National Trust's car park at grid ref: SX149513 provides easy access to a signposted walk where you can savour the delights of Pencarrow Head and Lantic Bay. We highly recommend you visit this beautiful stretch of coastline. Lantic Bay boasts a tempting beach which can be accessed with caution via an extremely steep path	

Starting outside The Old Ferry Inn, head uphill. You pass Marigold Cottage and The Blue Cottage on your left, a footpath on your left (not the one you want), St. John's Church on your right and, further up, the entrance to the inn car park also on your right. The lane goes round a bend after which you find a footpath on the right signed for Hall Walk, Pont and Polruan. Take this, passing the Old School House on your right.

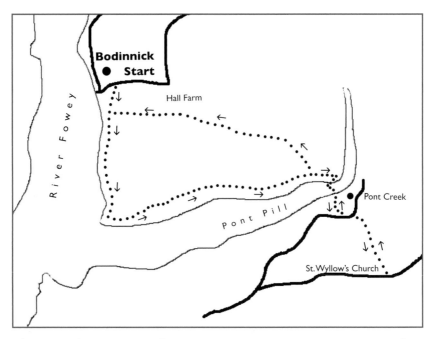

This delightful footpath, flanked by wild garlic in spring, has pretty views to the right over gardens and down to the village. Pass through a gate and continue, glancing down to the estuary where you may see the ferry wending its way. A National Trust sign shows that you are now joining the Hall Walk. Soon you reach a WWII memorial and from here the views across the estuary to Fowey are superb. Make the most of the benches.

Continue on the path and soon the view of Polruan, on the opposite side of the estuary to Fowey, opens up. The path passes a lovely National Trust shelter before arriving at the memorial to the writer, Sir Arthur Quiller-Couch, who lived in Fowey for over 50 years. Continue past his monument on this clear path. The water down to your right is Pont Pill and the path winds its way above this estuary through light woodland, abundant in spring with wild flowers: bluebells, red campion and stitchwort vying for space with the unfolding fronds of male and hart's tongue ferns.

At the end of the Hall Walk you reach a stile. Cross it and continue to a kissing gate about 20m further. Beyond this, walk along the bottom of the field with trees to your right. About 100m from the kissing gate you find a field gate on the right with a stone stile next it. Remember this point as you return here later.

Pass through the gate and descend on the woodland path beyond. Be cautious in wet weather as the rocky patches underfoot can be slippery. You drop to a crossing path, turn right here towards Polruan, you will see the buildings of Pont Creek below you which is where the mute swans hang out. Enjoy this lovely area – notice the old lime kiln across the water – then cross the footbridge and continue ahead, passing The Farmhouse, displaying its historic toll charges, and Pont Creek Cottage on your right. Here you will see a footpath sign directing you straight ahead for Polruan. Take this. Walk up away from the creek, ignoring the right turn for Polruan which you soon pass. Keep ahead and soon the path ascends steps

Mute Swan family at Pont Creek

Boats on Pont Pill

to join a lane. Go left here for about 10m then, as the lane bends left, take a track right, passing through a gate leading onto a footpath to the church. Follow this until you find the beautiful church of St. Wyllow. Explore here then retrace your steps all the way back to the footbridge at Pont Creek.

Re-cross the footbridge and ascend the footpath which you descended earlier, now signed for Bodinnick. A walk in the opposite direction is a different walk and this is a very nice stretch! Soon you reach a sharp left turn, take this and climb back up to the gate and stone stile. Beyond here is where your route changes. From the gate head diagonally left across the field to a gate in the top left corner, sparing a glance to the rolling hillside views behind as you climb.

Go left through this gate (there is an overgrown stile beside it) and now walk across the top of the next field with the boundary to your right. There are sweeping views round to your left, back towards St. Wyllow's church. Enter a second field and continue in the same direction, now with stunning views towards the estuary. Fowey and Polruan can be seen as you progress and, in the distance, the red and white daymark tower on Gribbin Head – the headland beyond Fowey. The tower was erected in 1832 as a navigation aid to shipping.

At the end of this second field go through the middle of three gates which is slightly to the right rather than straight ahead. This leads onto a track, descending in the same direction as before to a gate, beyond which you continue down on the track towards the buildings of Hall Farm. Just down here on the right look out for the stile leading into the area of the ruined Hall Chapel. This is an interesting spot to visit. The ruins have been well-preserved and are now clad in succulent wall pennywort.

Looking back to Polruan and the Fowey estuary

Hall Chapel

This ruined building is an unexpected surprise on the latter stages of the walk. Hall Chapel, one of only a few surviving mediæval chapels in Cornwall, was originally licensed as a private oratory in 1374–5 for the Mohun family. Formerly Barons of Dunster in Somerset (where they built Dunster Castle), they lived in a nearby manor house, now the site of the present Hall Farmhouse. They acquired the property in the early 14thC following their younger son's marriage to Elizabeth Fitzwilliam of Hall. The Chapel was built of local slate  from Pentewan, with the construction of the bell turret, which is still clearly visible today, following in the 15thC. After the Reformation, all domestic oratories fell out of favour and an inventory of 1620 indicates it was being used for domestic purposes rather than religious. In the 19thC the chapel housed a horse-powered threshing machine before later being converted to a cowshed. In 1926 the author and poet Geoffrey Grigson appealed for its preservation via an article in the Western Morning News. Despite this the building continued to decay and eventually the roof blew off during a storm in 1976 and the walls began to disintegrate. In 1997 successful efforts to reinforce the ruined chapel were made by the residents of Hall Farm.

From the chapel return to the track and continue down it to a gate. Go through and keep on in the same direction through the field, boundary to your right, leaving over a stile in the bottom corner. At this point you emerge back onto the path at the war memorial. Turn right here and retrace your steps the short distance back to the lane above The Old Ferry Inn.

Walk 3
St. Anthony Head

This is a route of reasonably easy walking on clear paths with no serious hills. The stunning coastal scenery gives way to tranquil creek-side walking along wooded paths and there are some rather lovely houses. In spring the route is steeped in wild flowers. Don't let the lack of refreshment stops en route put you off. It's a lovely walk.

Map: OS Explorer 105, Falmouth & Mevagissey 1:25 000
Start point: Porth Farm. Postcode: TR2 5EX. Grid ref: SW867329
Directions to start: St. Anthony is south of Gerrans, signposted off the A3078
Parking: There are a couple of National Trust parking areas near Porth Farm
Distance: 5¾ miles / 9.25km
Refreshments: None en route – take a picnic
Toilets: In the National Trust yard near the start and at St. Anthony Head
Nearby places to stay: Gerrans Bay House, Portscatho: 01872 580388
Nearby places of interest: St. Just-in-Roseland is a village renowned for its beauty and worth a visit. The church has one of the most idyllic settings imaginable; St. Mawes Castle (English Heritage): 01326 270526
Possible birds include: Blackbird, blue tit, carrion crow, chiffchaff, fulmar, gulls of various hues, linnet, magpie, pheasant, robin, shag, skylark, stonechat, swallow, whitethroat
Authors' tip: Take enough food for several picnics as there are many places along the way where it's pleasant to stop and wallow. Allow yourself time to visit the church at St. Anthony, it's a little gem

Emerge from the car park and across the road from Porth Farmhouse you will find a gate leading into a National Trust courtyard. The barns here house the loos and some information displays. From the courtyard a footpath leads to Towan Beach, take this and you are immediately rewarded with your first glimpse of the sea. This path leads right to the beach, but just before you reach it look out for the crossing coast path. You need to go right along here (unless you've gone for a paddle first), keeping the sea down to your left.

Follow the path as it rounds Killigerran Head after which you have a great view across Porthbeor Beach, reputedly one of the best in

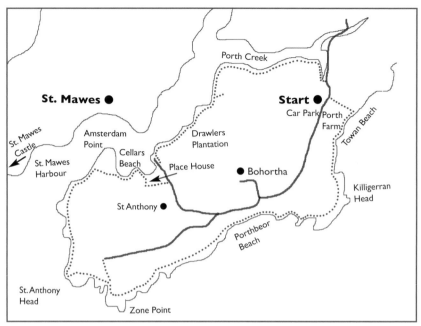

the area. As you continue look way across the sea to the far headland where you can see Lizard Lighthouse (Walk 4) on the most southerly point of mainland Britain and, inland, the former Satellite Earth Station at Goonhilly and the Bonythin Wind Farm. You will need clear conditions for these to be visible.

Almost ¾ mile from Killigerran Head you find a waymarker where you have an option to go inland towards the village of Bohortha. Ignore this and keep on the coast path, continuing to negotiate occasional stone stiles and sparing a glance back from time to time as the views are good in that direction too. When you reach a high point on the headland you will be able to see across the Fal Estuary to the town of Falmouth and Henry VIII's Pendennis Castle which guards the Carrick Roads (as the estuary is known) along with St. Mawes Castle on the east bank. You will be able to see the latter further on.

You reach the National Trust headland of Zone Point and beyond that St. Anthony Head where you will find interesting remnants of WWII activity and, thankfully, some public toilets. Above the buildings, on the coast path, you will find an orientation map on a stone plinth showing the features of the view around you. This is a superb spot and it was here that we met Graham, the Ordnance Survey's last remaining geodosy and positioning surveyor – what a wonderful job he has, covering a patch from The Scillies to Shetland!

Beyond this area you reach the car park, look out for a little path on the left which takes you steeply down to the lighthouse. A wonderful spot for a holiday cottage. Admire it, then turn your back and continue away from it along the coast path, the sea to your left and some quite exotic vegetation up to your right. You reach a large gate, continue beyond it and you begin to head up the estuary towards St. Mawes Harbour. This is a beautiful path with some magnificent, sentinel trees.

Approaching Porthbeor Beach

Looking back to Porthbeor Beach

Keep along the coast path and as you continue into the harbour the coast path swings inland for a stretch, skirting some woodland near Amsterdam Point and Cellars Beach. You are now heading towards the village of St. Anthony, keep on the signed coast path and soon you will see water reappearing down to your left. At the back gates to Place House go right, as signed, towards the Church and Place Quay.

The path skirts the magnificent Place House. At a fork go left, still on the coast path, signed for the church and ferry. This takes you down steps to the church – go in and sign their visitors' book, it helps their funding apparently. After this, continue along the path away from the church, passing a mediæval coffin which was discovered during the church restoration. Springtime wild flowers in this churchyard are one of the colourful highlights of the walk. The path leads to a lane, cross the stile and turn left to walk through the village of St. Anthony.

When you reach the quay look to your right to find a gate, beyond which you can join the coast path to the ferry (which is how the coast path gets across the water) and a footpath to Porth Farm, which is where you're heading. Continue through the National Trust land of Drawlers Plantation, you have lovely views down to the water on your left and the way is well-signed. Ignore any right turns for Bohortha and when the path starts to head along the banks of Porth Creek look out for the idyllically situated Quay Cottage on the opposite side. This stretch of walking is rich with bluebells during May. Soon the imposing sight of a house called Froe comes into view across the creek, where you may see resident swans. The path leads to a footbridge at the head of the creek. Cross this and turn right along a lovely, tree-lined path adjacent to the road, although at times it's hard to know a road is there as it's so concealed by vegetation. This final, idyllic stretch soon leads you back to Porth Farm.

Along the coast path beyond St. Anthony Lighthouse

Roseland Peninsula, Place and St. Anthony's Church

The Roseland Peninsula is a particularly beautiful part of an already lovely county. It derives from the Celtic word 'rhos' meaning gorse, which abounds in the area and gives a fabulous depth of colour to the glorious coastal scenery. The area is renowned for its picturesque villages and tranquil beaches. Savour it.

The remarkable Place House, the ancestral pile of the Spry family, occupies land once owned by an Augustinian Priory at Plympton in Devon. It is thought that the Norman doorway in the adjoining church was brought here from Plympton. The interior of the church is beautifully lit, with stained glass windows and glazed lights in the apex of the roof above the vaulting. Although the church was restored during the 19thC it retains its mediæval cruciform layout. It is now maintained by the Churches Conservation Trust.

St. Anthony's Church

Lizard & Kynance Cove

This reasonably easy walk is rich in bird and plant life. A particular attraction is the strong likelihood of seeing rare choughs which now breed on the cliffs hereabouts. When we were there youngsters had just fledged. The jewel in the crown as far as the route is concerned is the idyllic Kynance Cove where you may see seals while you sip tea at the beach café. The route is good for butterflies, we saw blues and meadow browns amongst many others, and wild flowers are abundant including the fabulously fleshy but very invasive pink and yellow Hottentot figs.

Map: OS Explorer 103, The Lizard, Falmouth & Helston 1:25 000

Start point: National Trust car park above Lizard Point. Postcode: TR12 7NT. Grid ref: SW704115

Directions to start: Follow the A3083 south from Helston into Lizard village and beyond

Parking: National Trust car park near Lizard Lighthouse, free to members if you show your card. There are other car parks but they are limited for space and duration

Distance: 6¼ miles / 10km

Refreshments: Ann's Pasty Shop, Lizard village: 01326 290889; Kynance Cove Beach Café: 01326 290436; Polpeor Café, Lizard Point: 01326 290939; Top House Inn, Lizard village: 01326 290974

Toilets: In the car park near the start, in Lizard village and at Kynance Cove

Nearby places to stay: Housel Bay Hotel, The Lizard: 01326 290417; Parc Brawse House, The Lizard: 01326 290466; Stormfield, The Lizard: 01326 290806

Nearby places of interest: Flambards, Helston: 01326 573404; Lizard Lighthouse Heritage Centre: 01326 290202

Possible birds include: Blackbird, buzzard, carrion crow, CHOUGH!!!, cormorant, fulmar, gannet, grey heron, gulls of various hues, house martin, house sparrow, jackdaw, kestrel, magpie, meadow pipit, oystercatcher, pied wagtail, raven, robin, rock pipit, shag, skylark, stonechat, storm petrel, swallow, turnstone, wheatear, whitethroat

Authors' tip: If you fancy an informal lunch, buy one of Ann's excellent pasties and make use of the picnic benches in the village centre

This is a large car park. Head towards the sea from your car and find the path which leads via steps and the coast path to Lizard

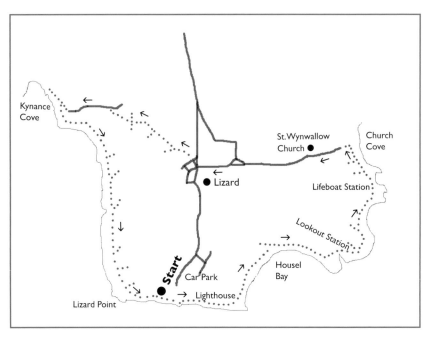

Point. You'll see a National Trust information board at the point where you exit the car park. Remember the route down as you'll need to retrace your steps at the end of the walk.

Spend a while at the Point. Here you are at England's most southerly tip and it is near here that choughs have their being. Youngsters had recently fledged and the RSPB had an information point when we were there. You may also see seals from here. When you've had your fill, return to the coast path and continue along it towards the Lizard Lighthouse with the sea down to your right, passing the steps you descended earlier from the car park. The path passes below the rather grand buildings of the lighthouse.

Keep on the coast path past Housel Bay, you will see the hotel on the cliff above it. When you reach a fingerpost with the option to head inland to the village, don't. Turn right to keep on the coast path and you soon pass the hotel up on your left. Ignore another option to go inland just beyond the hotel and continue along the coast, glancing back across this lovely bay for an excellent view of the lighthouse.

Eventually, as you round a bend in the path, the white, turreted building of the Lloyds Signal Station comes into view ahead. By some wooden huts you will see a right hand fork off the path leading out to a rocky promontory. Take this option to visit the crags then return along the other side of the promontory to rejoin the main coast path, passing the signal station and the National Coastwatch Institution Station. Beyond here the path continues past some absolutely idyllic cottages, Gone with the Wind and Bass Point House. About 100m after these look out for the yellow arrow directing you right to continue on the coast path.

The path rounds a promontory with a very large, prominent rock leaning above you to the left. Beyond that you are looking north

Housel Bay

up the coast towards Church Cove, Parn Voose Cove and beyond. Continue on the path past the Lifeboat Station, which was in a state of reconstruction when we went past. Continue until the path drops down to a three-way fingerpost by a tarmac lane. This indicates that you have walked 2 miles from Lizard Point. The coast path continues to Cadgwith but at this point you leave it and turn left inland up the lane to the village of Church Cove, passing some stunningly pretty thatched cottages on the way.

Eventually you pass the church of St. Wynwallow on your right and the lane leads you into Lizard village with its various amenities. Glance left towards the sea as you go – you will see the lighthouse which you passed earlier. On the way you will pass Ann's Pasty Shop which is a must!

From the village centre, near the car park, look out for the road sign pointing you to the coastal footpath. Follow its direction, passing the public loos on your left and just beyond these you will see another sign pointing you to Caerthillian and Kynance Coves. At the time of writing this was by a delightful jam stall, well-placed for some indulgence. The lane becomes a track and within 200m of the toilets you will see a public footpath on the right to Kynance Cove. Take this. In about 50m you will see a left fork with a public footpath sign, follow this past a bungalow to some stone steps. Ascend these and follow the elevated path beyond.

You reach descending steps beyond which you soon come across a fingerpost. Take the option going straight ahead. The path continues with more substantial, stepped stiles from time to time. This is a well-walked route and although signs are sometimes lacking the way is clear. You reach a tarmac road. Go straight ahead along it towards the car park, as indicated. The sea is away to your left and you pass a house called Carn Goon on your left. Any helicopter activity you may notice is down to the proximity to

RNAS Culdrose, one of Europe's largest helicopter bases – you will see its white 'golf ball' in the distance to your right.

The road leads to the car park above Kynance Cove. Bear right through the car park to find the path and steps down into this gorgeous cove where you will find a well-placed beach café from which you might see seals – we did. The cove is a good place for a paddle.

After refreshment retrace your steps towards the car park, but before you climb too far you will see a right hand option off the main path, which is the coast path to Lizard Point. Climb up, with Kynance Cove down to your right. The most scenic option from here is to hug the cliff-top path as much as possible on your way back. The dramatic view across the cove meets you as you proceed, with Asparagus Island just off the west headland and its accompanying rocks: The Bishop, Gull Rock and The Bellows.

Kynance Cove

Trinity House & Lizard Lighthouse

The corporation of Trinity House, whose remit is to aid the safety of shipping and seafarers, is a charity which received a Royal Charter from Henry VIII in 1514. This was granted to a fraternity of seafarers called The Guild of the Holy Trinity who regulated the pilotage of shipping in waters frequented by the King. Trinity House is best known for its  administration of the lighthouse system of England, Wales, the Channel Islands and Gibraltar but also provides other aids to navigation such as lightships, buoys and satellite navigation. It also licences and supplies Deep Sea Pilots who assist ships with navigation, and another, less familiar aspect of its work is the provision of retirement homes for ex-mariners.

Trinity House built its first lighthouse at Lowestoft in 1609 and over the centuries the appearance of these beacons was a welcome sight around our rocky shores. Accommodation for lighthouse keepers was within the tower of the lighthouse but in recent years the operation of the lights has become automated with the associated buildings frequently being turned into wonderfully-located holiday accommodation, as is the case at Lizard. The Lizard Lighthouse was built in 1751 with Trinity House taking over responsibility for it in 1771. The light was automated in 1998.

One of the authors spent a memorable evening at the top of a redundant, electricity-free lighthouse with a singer friend who was practising Ave Maria by torchlight for a wedding performance. The acoustics were superb.

Follow the path, for almost 2 miles, keeping the sea down to your right with lots of rocky coves and inlets and the village of Lizard ahead, slightly inland. At low tide the extensive Pentreath Beach is visible from the cliffs above and eventually you will once again see Lizard Lighthouse. You re-enter the National Trust headland of Old Lizard Point. Keep going along the coast, ignoring any paths heading inland, until you are back at Lizard Point. From here retrace your steps up the path and steps – the route you descended earlier. Your car awaits.

Helford River & Frenchman's Creek

Frenchman's Creek was made famous in Daphne du Maurier's novel of the same name and the latter stretch of the walk meanders along the shores of this peaceful creek which is particularly lovely at high tide. Prior to that you skirt the shores of the beautiful Helford River before crossing over to join the equally attractive Gillan Creek. Despite the drama and scenery this is relatively level walking with just a few gradients.

Map: OS Explorer 103, The Lizard 1:25 000

Start point: Helford. Postcode: TR12 6LB. Grid ref: SW759261

Directions to start: Helford is east off the A3083 which runs between Helston and Lizard

Parking: Car park near Down by the Riverside Café, Helford

Distance: 7 miles / 11.3km

Refreshments: Down by the Riverside Café, Helford: 01326 231893; New Inn, Manaccan: 01326 231323; South Café, Manaccan: 01326 231331; The Shipwrights Arms, Helford: 01326 231235

Toilets: Public toilets are situated at the starting point in the car park

Nearby places to stay: Gallen-Treath Guest House, Porthallow: 01326 280400 – although 4 miles from the start of the walk we stayed here and found it delightful. They are very accommodating for outdoor types! The Hen House in Tregarne, Manaccan: 01326 280236

Nearby places of interest: National Seal Sanctuary, Gweek: 0871 4232110. Trebah Garden, Mawnan Smith: 01326 252200

Possible birds include: Blackbird, chaffinch, collared dove, cormorant, curlew, gulls of various hues, house sparrow, jay, little egret, long-tailed tit, mute swan, pied wagtail, rook, woodpigeon, wren

Authors' tip: If timings permit take the ferry (Helford River Boats: 01326 250770) across Helford Passage to The Ferry Boat Inn: 01326 250625

Opposite the entrance to the café and car park a footpath sign leads you to a path under trees which heads for the coast path. You soon see the Helford River Sailing Club on your left. At the lane turn right passing a cottage on your left. This is The Old Pilchard Shed and this hamlet is Treath. The lane bends right and a fingerpost directs you forward onto a permissive coast path signposted to St.

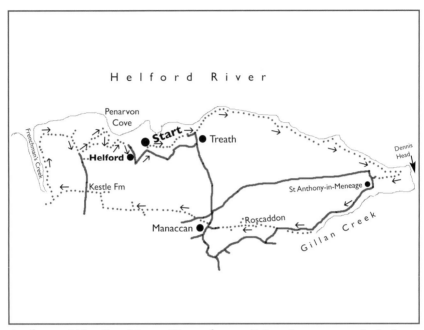

Anthony, 2½ miles. You will see the traditional acorn symbol along with the yellow arrow – this is now Bosahan Estate land.

Soon you reach a house which, at the time of writing, offered some interest in the form of a table selling beautifully coloured vintage bottles by way of an honesty box. Stay on the path as it bears right to pass the house on your left and then continues on its narrow passage through trees with the river on your left. There are occasional paths down to enticing, crystal-clear coves. Other than for exploration and a quick dip keep to the clearly marked coast path as it weaves through woodland.

At a kissing gate the path emerges into a field at which point turn left and continue with the hedge on your left. Pass through four fields some of which are linked by lovely old stone stiles. At the end of the fourth field the path heads up into another field, continue ahead and you'll soon notice that as well as the Helford Estuary on your left you are now joined by Gillan Creek on your right. Pass through a kissing gate and continue to a stile on your left. Cross here to explore Dennis Head, a circular path circumnavigates the area and Falmouth and St. Mawes can clearly be seen to the north. Return to the stile.

Once back at the stile turn right retracing your steps for about 30m and then bearing left round the field on the trodden path, savouring the views over Gillan Creek. The path leaves the field past a cottage and through a kissing gate. Walk ahead towards the church and turn left on the lane. This is St Anthony-in-Meneage. A fingerpost indicates that you're heading for Flushing. Keep on the lane as it passes Gillan Harbour on the left and continue for about ¾ mile until you reach a National Trust sign on your left for Gillan Creek. Take this path down to a wonderful viewpoint by a rather splendid tree then continue along until it rejoins the lane.

Press on along the lane for another 200m and at a left bend look out for a footpath on your right. Take this, it appears to bend back

Along the Helford River

Above Gillan Creek

on itself but then continues through woodland in the same direction and leads to the hamlet of Roscaddon. The path bends left into the hamlet and at the house of Little Roscaddon turns right signposted Manaccan. Continue ahead on the bridleway as you leave Roscaddon behind, ignoring a footpath to the right.

Enter the village of Manaccan passing a graveyard on your left. Continue ahead to the church and walk through the churchyard. At the T-junction turn left downhill to the pub (look out for the old well, restored for the 1977 Silver Jubilee) or right for South Café.

From South Café follow the lane as far as Minster Meadows. Go left here, there is a footpath sign for Helford, and after about 30m cross the stone stile onto a public footpath. This leads along a field with a hedge on your right. At a lane turn left for about 10m and then turn right to pick up another footpath across another stone stile. Walk ahead through the field on a well-trodden path to the opposite boundary, then turn left. Keep ahead until the path leaves the field beneath trees, crossing another stone stile. Within 400m you see a waymark post with a yellow arrow, keep straight ahead. In another 20–30m keep ahead at yet another marker. The path drops down to cross a stream with an impressive 'stepped' stile (or at least James was impressed!).

After a 100m turn left to cross a stile into a field, then turn right. Follow the boundary on your right to the end of the field where another yellow arrow directs you right. Continue through the next field with its boundary on your left to the top corner of the field where a fingerpost points you through the gate and straight ahead to Frenchman's Creek. Walk between the buildings of Kestle Farm to the lane, cross over and pick up the footpath opposite.

Keep on this path heading roughly west, you will spot a National Trust sign telling you when you enter the area of Frenchman's Creek. As the path bends left you will see a permissive path to the right, towards the creek. Take this, with the creek on your left, exploring the waterside as you go. The path takes you over a couple of little wooden footbridges and eventually takes a sharp right turn to head up some steps.

Frenchman's Creek

Daphne du Maurier's novel Frenchman's Creek, first published in 1942, is appropriately set in the idyllically romantic setting of this area of the Helford River during the reign of Charles II. If, like me, you were rather caught up by the story of English nobility being swept off its genteel feet by rakish French pirates you'll be as disappointed as I was when I heard it suggested that Frenchman's Creek is not actually deep enough to have accommodated Jean-Benoit Aubéry's ship. Pity. Oh well, back to realism – the walk is beautiful, let your imagination wander too.

When you meet a junction with the option to follow the creek-side path take this. This path eventually bends right away from the creek and leads to a metalled and grass drive. Turn right here and continue to the next junction where you turn right again, still on the permissive path and signed for Helford via Penarvon Cove. When you reach an almost-obliterated cattle grid go left at this junction signed for Pengwedhen and Helford via Penarvon Cove. At a fork keep right heading downhill for the cove.

At the cove walk across the back of the beach to pick up another footpath which takes you right off the beach and up through woodland. When you reach a T-junction go left downhill and at the bottom of the hill turn right past Popigale Cottage. Call in at The Shipwrights Arms (there really is no apostrophe!) then continue along the lane past the post office on your right. At the footbridge cross the river and go left uphill back to the car.

Beside Gillan Creek

Walk 6
Polzeath

This spectacular walk begins at the surfing resort of Polzeath. From here you soon ascend on to the cliffs where you'll witness some of the most dramatic scenery that the north Cornish coast has to offer. Whilst walking you will be treated to the constant accompaniment of surf-sound and skylarks.

Map: OS Explorer 106, Newquay & Padstow 1:25 000
Start point: Ann's Cottage car park, Polzeath. Postcode: PL27 6SR. Grid ref: SW935789
Directions to start: Polzeath is a small seaside town located on the Atlantic coast approximately 6 miles to the north west of Wadebridge
Parking: Ann's Cottage car park situated by the south-east side of the beach at Hayle Bay
Distance: 5¼ miles / 8.44km
Refreshments: Mowhay Café and Gallery, Trebetherick: 01208 816880; The Waterfront, Polzeath: 01208 869655
Toilets: In Polzeath
Nearby places to stay: St Moritz Hotel, Trebetherick: 01208 862242; The White Heron, Polzeath: 01208 863623
Nearby places of interest: Mowhay Café and Gallery, Trebetherick: 01208 816880; Porteath Bee Centre, St Minver: 01208 863718; Eden Project, Bodelva: 01726 811911
Possible birds include: Blackbird, buzzard, carrion crow, grey wagtail, gulls of various hues, house martins, house sparrow, jackdaw, kestrel, magpie, mallard, meadow pipit, rook, shag, skylark, stonechat, swallow, wheatear, whitethroat, woodpigeon, wren
Authors' tip: If you're feeling energetic why not try your hand at surfing. Surfs Up Surf School is close to the beach: 01208 862003

From the car park the walk begins (tide permitting) by crossing the back of the beach at Hayle Bay towards the headland of Pentire Point. Pass a beach café on your right and, about 100m from here, take the steps up off the beach. (If the tide is high follow the coast path along the road to this point.) At the top of the steps turn left along the path, below houses, with the beach and Padstow Bay down to your left. Look out for lizards on the path as we saw one

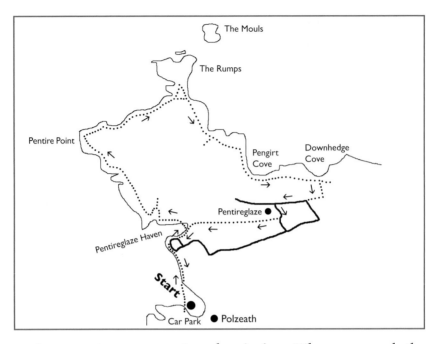

at close quarters, scampering ahead of us. When you reach the road turn left along it.

After a few metres of pavement you reach another trodden path heading across the grass towards the headland. This swings round to rejoin the road, passing a Dutch-gabled cream-coloured house on the left called Medla. Beyond this you'll see the coast path sign directing you to Port Quin via Pentire Point, 5 miles. Take this, soon passing the small beach of Pentireglaze Haven.

Looking west you can see two distinct headlands. Stepper Point in the foreground is topped by a stone tower, erected as a daymark to assist mariners with locating the entrance to the Camel Estuary. The second headland beyond is Trevose Head with its lighthouse.

When you meet an option to go right, don't. Keep left on the coast path towards Pentire Head, a mile from here. Enjoy this path, in

Approaching Pentire Head

Laurence Binyon

Few people will be unfamiliar with Binyon's poem For the Fallen, the third and fourth verses of which are so frequently used in Remembrance Day services. Although he originally hailed from Lancashire and studied at Oxford, it was on the cliffs at Pentire Head during a visit to Cornwall that

Binyon composed these memorable lines. By the time of the Great War he was too old to enlist but worked with the Red Cross in France. For the Fallen was written in 1914 and first appeared in The Times. Binyon published a great deal of poetry during his life. He died in Berkshire in 1943 during WWII, witness to the tragic fact that 'the war to end all wars' hadn't.

Looking towards The Rumps

spring its verges are fabulous with the flowers of thrift and birdsfoot trefoil.

When you reach the rocky promontory of Pentire Point you'll see the small island of Newland lying one mile to the north west. The path continues round Pentire Point, beyond this keep to the coast path with the wall to your right.

Just under 200m from Pentire Point you reach a bench with a fantastic view over the coastline towards The Rumps headland. It was here that Laurence Binyon's most famous poem, For the Fallen, was composed (see feature page 39). When you've had your fill of this very special place continue on the coast path.

Just prior to the path passing through a gate glance right to see a trig point – you are 83m above the sea. Continue, and when the path forks go left off the coast path out onto The Rumps. We recommend exploring this beautiful headland from which you'll see a path that loops back to rejoin the coast path.

Beyond The Rumps you'll see another right turn option, this time signed for Pentire Farm. Ignore this and continue. You are heading towards a lovely view over Port Quin Bay, the little island out to your left is The Mouls.

When you meet a waymarker showing a right hand option to the lead mines still keep ahead – the ongoing option towards Port Quin is what you need. Glance down just before this waymarker post for a dramatic view over Pengirt Cove.

Pass through a gate and continue on the coast path for about 600m towards Downhedge Cove. When you find another waymarker showing Pentireglaze to the right and Lundy Bay ahead, turn right

Coastline & The Mouls

away from the coast and onto National Trust land. Beyond the gate follow the fence to your left. At the far end of the field turn right to join a track, a yellow arrow guides your way through a gate and along the track. Look ahead now towards the building of Overhaven – it looks as if it's supporting the island out in the bay on its chimneys.

The track passes white cottages and emerges onto a minor lane. Continue ahead until a collection of houses is reached. This is Pentireglaze. East and West Cottages are high up to your right and Overhaven is to the left. At the time of writing these cottages were National Trust holiday lets. The lane swings left here soon passing barns on your left. A further 100m from here look out for a bridleway sign on the right and take it.

You're heading back to the coast now towards Pentireglaze Haven. The island visible ahead of you is Gulland Rock. The bridleway goes through fields. Keep ahead with a fence to your left, a valley to your right and the sea and island ahead of you. Leave the fields through a gate onto a track where, in 70m, you meet another track.

Go left here sweeping uphill. This path passes houses to reach Medla on the right, which we passed earlier. Turn right along the lane retracing your steps back to your car, Polzeath, paddling and pasties.

Overlooking Port Quin Bay

Walk 7

Treen & Porthcurno

This is one of the loveliest of walks. It passes some of the most beautiful, golden beaches you will find in Cornwall. The birds, particularly the gannets, are superb and there is a good chance of seeing seals. In spring and summer the wildflowers abound and around the theatre their exotic, cultivated cousins are quite spectacular – towering Echiums and squat, solid, spiky agave lend a very tropical feel to the area. This is one of those not-to-be-missed gems. The coast walking is quite rough – be well-shod.

Map: OS Explorer 102, Land's End 1:25 000

Start point: Treen. Postcode: TR19 6LG. Grid ref: SW394230

Directions to start: Treen is south of St. Buryan which is off the A30 between Penzance and Land's End

Parking: At the end of the village there is a field designated as a very reasonable pay and display car park

Distance: 4½ miles / 7.2km

Refreshments: The Logan Rock, Treen: 01736 810495; The Cable Station Inn, Porthcurno: 01736 810479

Toilets: Just outside the car park

Nearby places to stay: Ardensawah Farm, St. Levan: 01736 871520; Trendrennen Farm, Porthcurno: 01736 810585

Nearby places of interest: Minack Theatre, Porthcurno: 01736 810694; Porthcurno Telegraph Museum: 01736 810966

Possible birds include: Blackbird, blue tit, carrion crow, chaffinch, chiffchaff, gannet, goldfinch, gulls of various hues, house sparrow, jackdaw, magpie, pied wagtail, skylark, starling, swallow, whitethroat, wren

Authors' tip: If you have the opportunity and decent weather we highly recommend seeing a play at The Minack – but wrap up more warmly than you can ever imagine is necessary. Watching the aerial acrobats of gannets as they dive beyond the actors makes whatever production you are seeing more than memorable. Often there are matinees which might be incorporated into the walk. Alternatively, if there is no play on, you can pay to look round the theatre

Leave the car park, ignoring the footpath immediately left, and walk back along the lane, passing the phone box and post box on your left. After about 50m, the road bends right. Here leave the road and go left along the track forking almost immediately right

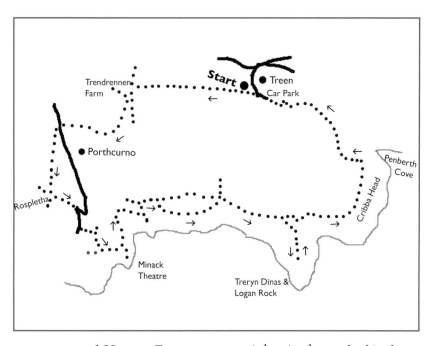

to pass round Houses Farm on your right. At the end of its barn there is a gate with a big stone stile beside it. Cross here and walk through the next two fields with the boundary to your left. In the third field keep straight ahead to a gap in the opposite boundary. Cross a stile into a fourth field and walk ahead, the sea is away to your left. Cross the next stile and then bear slightly diagonally left through a small field to another stile. Beyond this walk round two sides of the next field keeping the boundary on your right until you find a stile in the corner. Cross this to arrive in the yard of Trendrennen Farm.

Turn immediately left, keeping the buildings over to your right and the boundary to your left, and soon you reach a gate with footpath arrows. The direction you need is diagonally right along a clear track through three fields – this is well-signed with yellow arrows. At the end of the third field is a stile with a yellow footpath arrow. Follow its direction, bearing slightly right on the clear track, you can see the buildings of Porthcurno ahead and left. The track leads to a gate. Pass through and continue down the path beyond, you can see the enticing buildings of Porthcurno (the Inn) down to your left.

Descend to join a tarmac drive and turn right until you eventually reach a car parking area and beyond this the road through Porthcurno. Sea View House is opposite you. If you wish to go into the village go left, but the walk route follows the track leading off the opposite side of the road between houses. Cross the road and bear left along this track to a gate. Beyond this keep with the clear track – you can see the Museum over to your left and lovely views to the sea.

You reach the buildings of Rospletha, although there is nothing to tell you this when you get there. Follow the drive as it bears left around and then between the buildings (don't take any signed

Tempting beaches

footpaths off) until you reach the road. There are good views to Logan Rock across the bay as you proceed.

Turn right up the road and after about 50m go left down the drive to The Minack Theatre; this is a footpath. At the entrance into the theatre you will see a fingerpost with its acorn symbol directing you down onto the coast path. Take this, towards Porthcurno. The descent here is long, steep and involves rough steps – get your balance before you set off as you need your knees in low gear.

Your route on the coast path takes you round the back of Porthcurno Beach although paths lead onto it if you wish for a paddle. Follow the coast path up the cliffs, the sea to your right, and keep going until you pass a pillbox lookout. Eventually the path crosses a stile, beyond which you turn right – the coast path at this point is a bridleway. After about 200m a footpath goes right off the coast path, passing closer to the cliff. Take this as the views are better and you will pass a white pyramid, placed by the National Trust, to mark the end point of a telegraph cable which once ran between here and Brest. A little further on you will see a small pool in the verge to your left, the housing of a natural spring. The route follows the cliffs, although exploring beaches is an option if you wish – be cautious on the edges. The footpath ascends to rejoin the bridleway. You will see a path heading inland here but you turn immediately right and at the National Trust stone plinth bear right again, passing the plinth on your left. You are once more on a footpath running more or less parallel with a bridleway.

Eventually this leads up to rejoin the broad bridleway, turn right to continue with the sea to your right. About 50m further is a wide meeting of ways. A small granite waymarker post by a National Trust plinth indicates that the coast path now forks left, but first take the right fork to the headland of Treryn Dinas and the Logan Rock. This is a spectacular place, the site of an Iron Age 'ditch and rampart' cliff fort, so the detour off the coast path is very worthwhile, but, as always, exercise caution.

Return to the waymarker and continue on the coast path which now traverses Cribba Head towards Penberth Cove. Look along the coast towards Tater Du Lighthouse – a relatively young chap as far as lighthouses go. It was built in 1965 and has always been automated. The path drops into Penberth Cove, and if the tide is in and the sun is out the wave-wash over the boulders is lovely to see. Descend with the path until it lands you in the hamlet of Penberth. Turn left on the track towards a house about 50m away, passing right in front of it between the house and its garden to find the narrow path beyond. This does seem a bit intrusive but it is the way and is well-used – please respect the residents' privacy.

This idyllic little path heads inland, passing some school gardens on the right after which you fork left heading up through light

Looking towards Logan Rock

Minack Theatre

This open-air theatre, set into the cliff, is rather redolent of a Roman amphitheatre. With its sub-tropical rockery gardens it is a remarkable place to visit for sightseeing during the day or for one of its many performances.

'Minack' means 'rocky area' and this headland was bought by the creative Rowena Cade in the 1920s for £100. Here she built a house for herself and her widowed mother. Rowena's devotion to the performing arts had started at a young age and her sheer hard work, determination and vision ultimately gave birth to the theatre we see today. Shakespeare's The Tempest was the first production to be staged here in 1932, although at that time the Minack set-up was embryonic compared to the arrangements which developed over subsequent years. Rowena died in 1983, aged 90.

woodland to arrive at a stile. Cross this and follow the direction of the yellow arrow, passing through the field with the boundary to your right until you meet a stone stepped stile. Cross this and go through the next field, now with the boundary to your left. As the boundary turns left, keep ahead across the field, bearing slightly diagonally left to a gap in the far boundary. Here you will find a rather broken down stile crossing the bank. Beyond here continue across to another stile, beyond it turn right to follow round two sides of the field. You will see your start point just over the hedge. In the corner of the field a stile leads you onto a narrow path back into the village and the entrance to the car park.

Mouth of Rocky Valley (Walk 11)

Overlooking Chapel Porth (Walk 12)

Fowey estuary (Walk 2)

Churchyard spring flowers (Walk 3)
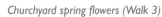

Overlooking Helford River (Walk 5)

Looking towards Trebarwith Strand (Walk 1)

St. Anthony's Lighthouse (Walk 3)

Porthcurno beaches (Walk 7)

Coastline nr Trevaunance Cove (Walk 12)

Housel Bay (Walk 4)

The Rumps & Mouls Rock (Walk 6)

Seal watching on The Carracks (Walk 8)

Overlooking Gull Rock & Trebarwith Strand (Walk 1)

Talland Bay (Walk 9)

Waterfall, Rocky Valley (Walk 11)

The Cheesewring (Walk 10)

Looe Island (Walk 9)

Boscastle Harbour (Walk 11)

Kynance Cove (Walk 4)

Zennor

There is a great sense of the ancientness of Cornwall during this walk, from the route's proximity to ancient burial chambers and the location of the churchyard on an Iron Age site to the more recent 13thC pub. There are excellent vantage points for watching seals on the outward coastal route, and the return journey through a succession of small fields along the 'coffin' path is quite delightful. When we walked this in June we saw masses of six-spot burnet moths. The coastal section can be very rough going and 'bouldery' but don't be put off. We've known this route for about 20 years and it's still a favourite.

Map: OS Explorer 102, Land's End 1:25 000	
Start point: St. Senara's Church. Postcode: TR26 3BY. Grid ref: SW454384	
Directions to start: Zennor is just off the B3306, west of St. Ives	
Parking: There is a very reasonably priced car park in the middle of the village	
Distance: 5¾ miles / 9.25km	
Refreshments: The Old Chapel Café, Zennor: 01736 798307; The Tinners Arms, Zennor: 01736 96927	
Toilets: Near the car park	
Nearby places to stay: The Gurnard's Head, nr Zennor: 01736 796928; Tregeraint House, nr Zennor: 01736 797061	
Nearby places of interest: Geevor Tin Mine, Pendeen: 01736 788662; Tate, St Ives: 01736 796226; Wayside Folk Museum, Zennor: 01736 796945; Barbara Hepworth Museum & Sculpture Garden: 01736 796226	
Possible birds include: Blackcap, buzzard, chaffinch, chiffchaff, dunnock, fulmar, goldfinch, great tit, gulls of various hues, house sparrow, jackdaw, kestrel, long-tailed tit, magpie, pied wagtail, shag, skylark, swallow, whitethroat, wren	
Authors' tip: If you have time and energy go up on Zennor Hill to seek out the ruined megalithic burial chamber of Zennor Quoit. This is at grid ref: SW468380. It can be accessed via a track off the B3306 about a mile to the east of Zennor at grid ref: SW468387. From the road to the quoit and back is a round trip of just over a mile. There is nowhere to park along the road so you need to walk from the village	

Walk out of the village passing the church of St. Senara on your right. At the end of the church wall follow the sign which points you left towards the coast along a broad path. Follow this and the

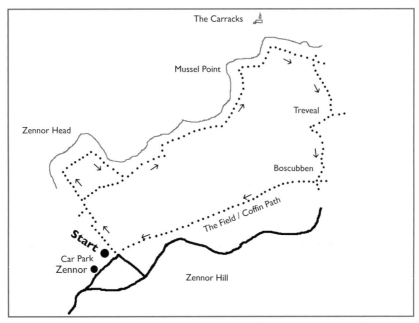

tarmac soon gives way to a narrow path, still going in the same direction towards the coast. Beyond a stone stile the path forks. Take the coast path option ahead towards St. Ives, keeping the sea down to your left. This route will take you round the coastline of Zennor Head. Glance left as you go to the headlands west of here, the distinctive, jutting Gurnard's Head is clearly visible as resembling the fish for which it is named.

When you reach the rocky outcrop at Zennor Head, look out for the National Trust plaque indicating that they received this donation of land in 1953. Continue and the path leads up to a crossing path. Turn left and keep going – you are now traversing Tremedda Cliff with glorious coastal views in both directions, the tide-smoothed rocks below resembling vast bread rolls. Keep with the coast path and its yellow-arrowed, acorn waymarkers, ignoring any option to turn inland. You pass the headland of Carn Porth and just beyond this cross a spring with its crystal pool and small waterfalls.

Mussel Point is reached just over 1½ tough miles after leaving Zennor Head. There's nothing to indicate the name when you get there but the craggy islands out to sea are The Carracks and these, together with the coastline rocks, are good places for seal-watching. Tarry a while. The cove between Mussel Point and The Carracks bears the intriguing name of Economy Cove.

Beyond here the path leads you along the top of Treveal Cliff. A little further on a granite plinth tells you that you're 3 miles from Zennor and at this point (River Cove) you turn right, inland, to take the field path back to Zennor. Keep on this lovely verdant path, you can hear the stream down to your left, until it emerges at the gate to Trevail Mill. Turn right along the drive away from the Mill.

You reach the buildings of Treveal where you will find another granite plinth on your right. Bear left with the track, signed for Zennor along the field path and leave Treveal behind you,

Towards Gurnard's Head

Zennor

Zennor is a remote granite-built village set in a hollow on the Penwith peninsula. St Senara's Church has a typical Cornish barrel roof, but of most interest is the so-called Mermaid Chair incorporating mediaeval bench ends carved over 500 years ago. One shows a mermaid holding a looking glass and a comb. Legend says she visited the church many times to listen to the chorister Matthew Trewhella, who enchanted her with his singing. When their eyes finally met they instantly  fell in love and she lured him away one night into the sea at Pendour Cove. It is said that if you visit this location on a calm summer evening you may hear Matthew singing faintly on the breeze.

Zennor Quoit is a prehistoric burial chamber, one of many similar tombs to be found in Cornwall. It may originally have been topped by a cairn or mound and the massive capstone you see today slipped from its original position in 1861 when a local farmer attempted to remove stones to make a cow shed. The timely intervention of the local vicar prevented the quoit from being completely dismantled. The nearby upright posts are possibly the beginnings of this un-completed construction. Zennor was a 'portal' quoit, having a porch through which the chamber could be entered. Ancient pottery remains have been found at the site.

The English novelist D. H. Lawrence moved to Zennor with his German wife, Frieda, in March 1916 staying at Tregerthen Cottage. As WWI progressed anti-German feeling was rife, and locals turned against their new residents. Amongst accusations of spying and signalling to German submarines the couple finally received an order to leave the county by 15 October 1917, under the Defence of the Realm Act.

continuing until you reach Boscubben on your right. A fingerpost sends you straight on (left is back to the road) along a clear tarmac track with expansive views to the sea away to your right.

Soon you reach the idyllically situated Wicca. A clear sign directs you between the buildings towards a succession of small fields. About 20m beyond the house cross the first stone stile and go through the first field. This leads quickly to a second stile and thence to a third big, stone stile. Keep ahead after this to the far boundary where you will find horizontal stones, effectively a sheep/cattle grid. Beyond this follow the direction of the yellow arrow through the field, ensuring you keep in a straight line, don't veer right on the animal-trodden path. Leave this field via another stone grid within 150m of the last one, beside an arrowed post.

This leads to a narrow path which wends its way to a ruined chapel, originally built by Methodists in 1850. The path beyond the chapel is clear, keep straight ahead, avoiding any veerings off, until you reach Lower Tregerthen Farmhouse on your right. Beyond here cross their drive and continue on the path which runs into a field. Keep the boundary on your right through two small fields and then straight through the middle of a third. Just keep ahead until you reach Tremedda Farm on the right. A waymarker here points you straight on, crossing the drive and following the next field boundary on your right.

Path off Zennor Head

Keep straight on through more small fields, the path is well-trodden and the rooftops of Zennor start to appear ahead with the church tower over to the left. Keep to the path with its successive stone grids which help to keep you on the right route as you return to the village. The path gradually swings left to aim for the church, and brings you back to the point at which you started. You have been following the route along which the local departed might have been carried on their final trip to the church, hence the expression 'coffin path'. What a lovely way to go.

Field path back towards Zennor

Talland Bay & Polperro

*One of the authors has been holidaying in this area for over 20 years –
and he lives less than 70 miles away, so this is quite a commendation.
Looe is a beautiful town although this isn't on the route of the walk. The
walk itself starts along one of the loveliest stretches of south Cornish
coastline and passes through a classic fishing village. The return part of
the walk is on quiet country lanes with rewarding views and requires
some steep ascents.*

Map:	OS Explorer 107, St. Austell & Liskeard 1:25 000
Start point:	National Trust car park near Hendersick Farm on the lane between Portlooe and Talland. Grid ref: SX236520
Directions to start:	Talland Bay is situated between Looe and Polperro off the A387
Parking:	National Trust car park near Hendersick Farm
Distance:	5¾ miles / 9.25km
Refreshments:	Polperro and Looe have plentiful, varied places to eat. Additionally there is The Smugglers Rest Beach Café, Talland: 01503 272259 and Talland Bay Beach Café, 01503 272088
Toilets:	Public toilets are situated at Talland Bay and in Polperro
Nearby places to stay:	Talland Barton Farm, Talland Bay: 01503 272429; Talland Bay Hotel: 01503 272667 plus a range in surrounding villages and towns
Nearby places of interest:	The Eden Project, Bodelva: 01726 811911; Paul Corin's Music Machines, St Keyne: 01579 343108; the Looe Valley Railway – contact Looe Tourist Information: 01503 262072; Woolly Monkey Sanctuary, Murrayton nr. Looe: 01503 262532
Possible birds include:	Blackbird, blackcap, blue tit, buzzard, carrion crow, chaffinch, chiffchaff, cormorant, fulmar, goldcrest, goldfinch, great tit, green woodpecker, gulls, house sparrow, jackdaw, kestrel, magpie, oystercatcher, pied wagtail, raven, robin, skylark, stonechat, swallow, woodpigeon, wren
Possible insects include:	Fritillary, common blue, red admiral and speckled wood butterflies; six spot burnett moth
Authors' tip:	If you have time take a boat trip around Looe Island. Several companies in Looe run these and they make for an enjoyable jaunt.

From the end of the car park take the footpath down through the
trees. When the footpath meets a track cross diagonally to the right
to pass through another footpath gate. Continue until you reach

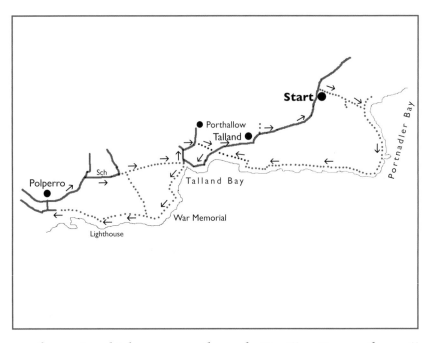

another gate which you pass through. You'll notice on the wall ahead a sign which reads "footpath to cliffs keep near the hedge please close the gate." Turn right here heading towards a barn. Pass through several gates keeping the boundary on your left as you walk downhill along this permissive path towards the coast. Looe Island, also known as St George's Island, starts to become clearly visible as the coastal view opens up spectacularly before you. Keep on this path as it winds down to join the coast path above Portnadler Bay. Turn right here and continue along the coast path heading west towards Talland Bay along National Trust coastline. For the ornithologists amongst you it is certainly worth scanning the little rocky islets down below for bird life.

As the path veers right into Talland Bay keep to the lower narrow path that leads you to the entrance of the Smugglers Rest – a nice spot to refresh and watch the sea. From here continue along the lane down to Talland Bay, passing the public loos, to another beach café. Continue on the coast path beyond here steeply uphill for about 100m. The coast path then turns left off this path and, thankfully, flattens out somewhat to give you time to recover. Views to the left and behind over Talland Bay and its variegated rock formations are worthwhile. Keep on the acorn-signed coast path passing Westcliff Old Court. In approximately 500m you reach the War Memorial, raised to the memory of soldiers from Talland and Polperro who died during the two world wars. Nearby is a stone bench which in turn is in memory of Florence Jerram who donated the stone cross.

Proceed along the coast path and after a ¼ mile or so beyond the War Memorial keep a lookout for the dinky lighthouse that nestles on the cliffs beyond and below you. It looks like a salt pot.

This approach to Polperro is the best way to arrive. Had you driven to this jewel of Cornwall you would have been greeted by

Coastline at Portnadler Bay

Talland Bay Smugglers

The area of Talland Bay, like most of the Cornish coast, is steeped in smuggling lore and legend, fact and fabrication interwoven. The 18thC was a busy time for smugglers, or 'free traders' as they were known, who shipped in illicit spirits, tea and baccy from Europe. Endeavouring to dodge the 'Preventive Men', their boodle was moved inland  under cover of darkness, at times, allegedly, via the village church, and tales of spirits of a different kind abound. Smuggling was very much a community activity and it is thought that by the end of the 18thC half a million illegal gallons of brandy were passing through Cornwall every year. Convicted smugglers could, at best, hope for transportation as a preferable alternative to being hanged. Interestingly the area was also the scene of similar activity during the 20thC, a drug smuggling ring being uncovered here in 1979.

Polperro

an enormous car park and an arduous trek down to the centre of the village. By this route the first glimpse of this fishing village is a classic picture-postcard view and a fitting way to begin your exploration.

Keep on the lane down into the village admiring picturesque cottages en route. In particular look out for The Shell House which you pass on your right. Take time out in Polperro – explore the village, the beach with its sea cave and Chapel Cliff with rewarding views over the harbour.

After exploring Polperro seek out the Post Office on Fore Street. If you're facing the Post Office your route lies uphill to the right. As the road forks go left up Talland Hill – bring oxygen! This lane continues steeply uphill and after approx 0.3 mile take a right turn (signed for the coast path) which leads you past a school and residential area. When the road bends left keep ahead on a tarmac lane called Sand Hill. Ahead of you is a footpath sign – don't take this back down to the coast but keep ahead. There is a good panorama from here over Talland Bay and beyond that stretching as far as the Rame Peninsula. Keep descending to Talland Bay at which point retrace your steps as far as the telephone box. At this point, continue ahead uphill for about ¼ mile until you reach a footpath on your right. This is just before the Talland Bay Hotel. Take this footpath and enjoy more stunning views as you descend to The Smugglers Rest. From here follow the lane eastwards rather than returning to the coast path. It will lead you uphill past the church of St. Tallan and Talland Barton Farm. The car park from whence you started is ¾ mile from the church.

Bodmin Moor & the Cheesewring

Perched on the south east corner of Bodmin Moor, Minions, at 1,000 feet above sea level, is the highest village in Cornwall. Once one of the most productive copper mining areas in the world, ruined workings abound as testament to a bygone age. The Hurlers Stone Circles and Cheesewring rock formations are mysterious attractions to an already spectacular landscape. This is generally level walking with far-reaching views, but there is one fairly steep descent where you'll need to get your knees in gear. The ponies that you see on this walk graze wild but are owned.

Map: OS Explorer 109, Bodmin Moor 1:25 000

Start point: Minions. Postcode: PL14 5LE. Grid ref: SX262713

Directions to start: Minions is signed off the B3254, Launceston to Liskeard road

Parking: The car park is on the north east side of Minions, clearly shown on the OS map. It's by the road sign for Sharp Tor and Henwood

Distance: 5¾ miles / 9¼km. This can easily be split into two separate walks – see text below

Refreshments: Cheesewring Hotel, Minions: 01579 362321; Hurlers Halt, Minions: 01579 363056. Minions Tearooms: 01579 363386. Wheal Tor, Caradon Hill: 01579 363401

Toilets: In Minions village

Nearby places to stay: Cheesewring Hotel, Minions: 01579 362321; Wheal Tor, Caradon Hill: 01579 363401

Nearby places of interest: Carnglaze Caverns, St Neot: 01579 320251; Eden Project, Bodelva: 01726 811911; Siblyback Lake Country Park, near Liskeard: 01579 346522; Sterts Open Air Theatre, Upton Cross: 01579 362382

Possible birds include: Blackbird; buzzard; carrion crow; chaffinch; cuckoo; house martin; jackdaw; kestrel; magpie; pied wagtail; raven; redstart; skylark; starling; swallow; willow warbler; yellowhammer

Authors' tip: If time allows, an additional treat is to take a 3½ mile drive to the car park at Draynes Bridge (grid ref: SX227689). From here you can take the short riverside ramble along the Fowey as it wends its way through beautiful woodland to the tranquil and picturesque Golitha Falls

Note: Be aware: part of this route is across open moorland, so a map and compass are needed – and clear weather conditions

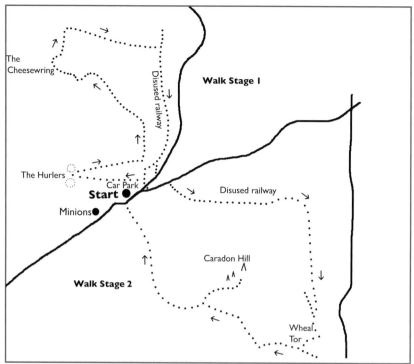

Before setting off get your bearings by first taking a glimpse at the information boards in the car park. To the south east of here you will see Caradon Hill and its transmitters, the highest of which is a staggering 238m (780 feet). To put this into perspective that's 61m (200 feet) taller than the BT Tower in London. You're usually well served for a mobile phone signal on this walk! Another more distant landmark is Kit Hill which is due east of Caradon. The 'toothpick' point on its summit is the chimney of Kit Hill Great Consols Mine, built in 1858.

Find the fingerpost in the top left hand corner of the car park, away from the road. Take the sign for The Hurlers along the trodden path. The two stone circles are only 400m away and soon come into view. Reach them and explore – it's a magical and mysterious place (see feature page 65). On a clear day you also have a good view of the Cheesewring rock formation to the north. You'll soon be heading there but, before you do, head towards the old mine building to the east (and just north of the car park from whence you started). This is now the Minions Heritage Centre and is located in the restored engine house of the South Phoenix Mine. It's well worth a visit.

Exit the Heritage Centre and follow the direction of its steps north along a clear track directly towards Stowe's Hill and the Cheesewring. You meet a couple of fenced areas en route which you can skirt around quite easily. As you approach Stowe's Hill the views around get ever more impressive. The immediate landscape is rather reminiscent of Sir Arthur Conan Doyle's Lost World and the search for the plateau.

Soon you approach a reconstruction of Daniel Gumb's Cave, a mystic and mountain philosopher who lived nearby with his

View from Stowe's Hill

family in the 18th century amid the natural granite blocks. Ascend beyond this to a fence. Follow its line skirting a disused quarry to your right (popular with rock climbers). Clamber up to the Cheesewring and admire it. Continue to the peak of Stowe's Hill observing all the other natural rock formations around. This is a special place. The views from here on a clear day are superb. 7½ miles to the northwest you can see Brown Willy, at 420m above sea level, the highest point on Bodmin Moor. You are standing at 375m, so you're quite high too! Just over ½ mile to the north you can see Sharp Tor and the village of Henlade below to its right. Looking east you can see into the neighbouring county of Devon and the hills and tors of Dartmoor. Caradon Hill and Kit Hill lie to the south east and, between them, Plymouth Sound might be visible 18½ miles away.

Head to the east(ish) side of Stowe's Hill where a large rock signifies your escape route through the stones, these are the remains of a Bronze Age defence wall which surrounded the settlement of Stowe's Pound. Head down this steep hill with caution in the direction of Cheesewring Farm, which can be seen below you. There's a good range of plants as you descend – look out for tormentil and stitchwort.

When you reach the wall by the farm turn right along the footings of an old disused railway. There are fantastic views along here. It's not like a railway line at all, more like a series of granite stepping stones – really good fun. As you advance the Cheesewring makes a final appearance behind peeking to say goodbye.

Continue along the track passing South Phoenix Farm on your left and continue back to the car park.

For the second stage of this walk leave the car park onto the tarmac lane and take the 2nd left signposted for Upton Cross and Rilla

Mill. Watch out for traffic. After 125m, and just before you reach the stanchions of a dismantled railway bridge, turn right up a distinct path leading off the lane. This trodden path leads up onto a broad disused railway embankment which circles its way round Caradon Hill in a clockwise direction. You pass some moody mine ruins, now very much an organic part of the landscape. The fantastic views continue towards Kit Hill and the more distant hills of Dartmoor to the east.

Eventually the old railway curves and you'll see the road below you to the left (B3254). When you approach a disused mine look up to the right where you'll see a pine copse which surrounds Wheal Tor, at 996m above sea level, the highest inn in Cornwall.

Continue along the path keeping parallel to the road until you reach a disused mine tip, which you keep on your right. Here the path bends right away from the road. The track meets another

Leaving Stowe's Hill along the old railway

Cheesewring and The Hurlers

The Cheesewring is a natural rock formation of granite slabs formed by weathering. It is situated on Stowe's Hill and gets its name due to the piled slabs resembling a 'cheesewring', a press-like device that was used to make cheese. The stone rings, one on top of the other, reach a height of 32 feet and seem to defy gravity. During operations at the neighbouring quarry this magnificent natural structure was reinforced for fear of toppling during blasting.

The Hurlers are a group of three stone circles, thought to have been built circa 1500BC. They are positioned in line running north to south with the southern-most circle being incomplete. According to local superstition they attained their name after the ancient Cornish game of hurling. Legend has it that these were people who were transformed to stone after breaking the rules of the Sabbath by daring to play the game on a Sunday. To the west of the circles are two separate standing stones known as The Pipers. In pre-Roman times Druids may have staged rituals and sacrifices here.

broad crossing track and to your left you'll notice a parking area. Turn right here. As we approached Wheal Tor we saw the welcome sight of a Sharp's Doom Bar lorry emerging post-beer delivery. Visit Wheal Tor – we did! We found a very warm welcome and the views from the inn's elevated position don't disappoint.

Stagger back to the entrance gate of the inn and turn right. Follow the tarmac track away from the periphery of the grounds with the dominant mast of Caradon Hill ahead of you. The track continues to a private house but, before reaching this, veer off left across the moor on a trodden path keeping the transmitters to your right. This is a steady uphill drag with a stone wall to your left keeping you company. Pause for breath and enjoy the fabulous views behind you across Wheal Tor and beyond.

As you reach the brow of the hill you'll see the village of St Cleer down to your left and ahead of you the familiar territory that you walked earlier. Stowe's Hill and the Cheesewring can be seen, as can Sharp Tor, Minions, the Minions Heritage Centre and the car park. The path across the moor joins a tarmac drive. Keep following this as you descend to the village. Once you reach the Minions Shop and Tearooms turn right for 150m to the car park.

Golitha Falls (see authors' tip, page 60)

Boscastle & Rocky Valley

This walk has been one of our favourites for many years. It has everything: superb coastline, lovely woodland, tranquil riverside walking, a coastal gorge and some interesting history along the way. The terrain can be rough in places so be well-shod.

Map: OS Explorer 111, Bude, Boscastle & Tintagel 1:25 000
Start point: Boscastle. Postcode: PL35 0HE. Grid ref: SX099912
Directions to start: Boscastle is at the junction of the B3233 and B3266 and is clearly signed off the A39
Parking: There is an extensive car park clearly signed in the village
Distance: 8 miles / 12.9km
Refreshments: Boscastle is well-provided with places to eat. There is a vast array of inns / tea rooms and restaurants from which to choose
Toilets: Public toilets are situated in the car park
Nearby places to stay: Bossiney Farm Campsite, Bossiney: 01840 770481; Tredole Farm, Trevalga: 01840 250595; Trerosewill Farmhouse, Paradise: 01840 250545
Nearby places of interest: Tintagel has a plethora of interesting sites, including the ruined legend-rich castle: 01840 770328
Possible birds include: Buzzard, carrion crow, chaffinch, chiffchaff, cormorant, dipper, fulmar, goldfinch, great tit, gulls of various hues, jackdaw, kestrel, magpie, oystercatcher, raven, robin, rook, shag, skylark, stonechat, swallow, wheatear, whitethroat, woodpigeon, wren
Authors' tip: If visiting at a time when access to St. Nectan's Glen Waterfall is permitted we would strongly recommend you do so

From the car park turn left along the road towards the harbour. At the head of the harbour, keep bearing left until you find yourself climbing up Old Road. Although steep, this hill has some beautiful cottages to admire on the way up. At the top of the road (by now it's Fore Street) go straight across, continuing up High Street to pass The Napoleon Inn on your right. A short distance beyond this notice the fabulous chimneys with the 'witches seats' on the Old Brigg Inn (now a holiday cottage). These seats were meant to keep them happy and dissuade them from coming down the chimneys. Beyond here turn right along Paradise Road.

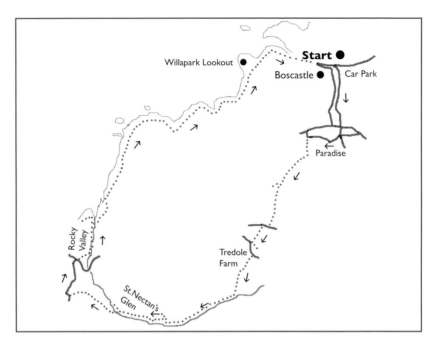

This road bends a bit and passes Paradise House on your left. Finally the road bends right to re-join the main road, but don't go right. At this point, on your left, you will see a yellow-arrowed footpath along a lane which you take. Keep ahead, passing Trerosewill Farm on your left. The lane bends right, then left and just after this left turn you will see a footpath on the right over a stile. Take this and walk straight up the field to a stile which you can see ahead. From here follow the direction of the yellow arrow across the next field to the gap which is visible in the far boundary. Here cross the stile and continue with the boundary on your left. As this left boundary ends keep ahead in the same line to a gate on the far side of the field. Coastward views here are dominated by the church above Boscastle and an intriguing bright white 'folly' – you will be up there later.

Beyond the gate go left along the hedge to some steps and a stile. Beyond here bear right up the next field to a stile which you can see in the fence. Cross this stile and continue uphill in the same line which will bring you to a gate in the top right hand corner of the field. Pass through here and you will see another footpath gate a few metres away leading onto a track. Yellow arrows help guide you through this junction. Follow the track to the lane and turn right along it. After 100m you will find another footpath on the left, adjacent to a track. Take this footpath over the stile (don't go along the track) and follow the direction of the sign pointing you diagonally left across the field. Enjoy sweeping views as you go, the sea is to your right. In the bottom corner of the field exit onto the lane and turn left towards Tredole Farm. After its garden follow the footpath off to the right which tells you you're heading for St. Nectan's Glen in 1 mile. This passes through the buildings of Tredole, following a narrow, fenced path.

This narrow path soon ends and you keep ahead to join a track. There are lovely views across the valley here. When the track

St. Nectan's Glen

Exploring a scary side path

emerges into a field go diagonally left down the field as shown by the arrow. This leads to a stile by a gate. Beyond here you will find a little, narrow path passing downhill between hedges. Follow this, you soon see a path going left which you ignore. Continue downhill, passing a ruined cottage on the left and arriving at a stream. This idyllic, verdant area is worth a linger before turning right to follow the stream to your left.

The small fields through which you now pass are awash during the spring with the pink flowers of lady's smock and the yellow of celandine and primrose. In the boundaries you may also spot dog's mercury – an indicator of the site of ancient woodland. Savour this area, following the clear path beside the stream until you reach an idyllically situated house called The Hermitage. During the summer this private garden is opened to the public to enable you to visit the waterfall at St. Nectan's Kieve. Follow the path to the garden gate where you will see two footpath arrows. Take the one which directs you left off the track. This goes down steps to descend on a narrow path beside the woodland garden, with dappled views down into the glen and the music of the waterfall accompanying you. This is a lovely, sylvan path which passes another overgrown ruined cottage and keeps dropping to eventually meet the stream.

Follow the water through this beautiful glen, crossing a couple of footbridges until you meet a three-way fingerpost beside a third bridge. Take the option across the bridge towards Halgabron. This leads away from the stream and eventually enters a field. The yellow arrow here indicates that your way lies diagonally left across the field with houses over to your right. You reach a stile onto a lane, along which you turn right, heading for the coast.

Follow this quiet lane for about 0.3 mile. Along here we found a tiny mouse sitting in the road, partaking of squashed snail. He was so engrossed that it was some time before he noticed us, despite James walking right over him. Very dear. The lane meets the Boscastle-Tintagel road. Cross it and take the footpath down the drive opposite signed for the coast path via Rocky Valley. This path passes the buildings of Trevillet Mill and about 50m from the road the footpath is signed right over a footbridge. Take this and follow it through Rocky Valley to the ruins of Trewethett Mill and the labyrinth carvings. Look out for the old quoin stone amongst the ruins.

Cross the water and follow the river on your right. Continue along the path seaward (passing a footbridge – remember this for later) as far as you can safely go to experience the full drama at the mouth of Rocky Valley. The limpet-bejewelled rock faces near here are spectacular and this is, without doubt, a Cornish highlight. Once you've had your fill of this wonderful place retrace your steps to the footbridge passing a spectacular waterfall en route. A

Coastline towards Boscastle

Rocky Valley Maze Carvings

Carved into the rock face near the ruined Trewethett Mill, these classical 'labyrinth' carvings are of uncertain age. Previously covered by vegetation, they were discovered by a local man in 1948 and were originally thought to be Bronze Age. There has since been speculation on this with some authorities dating them at just a few hundred years old. Many theories surround the origin of the carvings, some linking them with an early Christian hermitage which may have existed in St. Nectan's Glen, others with former tenants of the mill....the jury is very much out as far as their true age and meaning are concerned. Whatever its enigmatic history this rock art is fascinating. The labyrinths are of quite fine construction and were probably carved with a metal tool rather than stone. They hold an appeal for all who pass by and have become something of a Mecca for modern-day pagans.

yellow arrow directs you across the bridge signed to Boscastle, 2¾ miles. The path climbs steeply out of Rocky Valley. In spring and early summer this area and the surrounding coastline is glorious with flowers: thrift, sea campion, primrose, violet, stitchwort, celandine, bluebell, squill and tormentil amongst many others. The yellow of gorse flowers can be incredibly vibrant against a blue sky. It takes your mind off the climb.

Keep on the coast path towards Boscastle, don't be tempted to turn right inland. You will see the acorn waymarker from time to time to guide you along. Sightings of seals are regularly reported along this section of coast and also the occasional dolphin, so keep your eyes peeled. Seabirds abound on the craggy ledges.

You'll get occasional glimpses of the bright white folly mentioned earlier which you'll be visiting soon. Continue on the coast path entering the National Trust area of Forrabury and after this, before the coast path begins to descend into Boscastle Harbour, go left through the gate up to the white lookout tower. Glance behind at this point to see a church peeking over the hillside at you. There are lovely views of the harbour down to the right as you ascend to the tower. This is Willapark Lookout and was built in the early 19thC by a local landowner as a summerhouse. It was later leased to the Board of Trade as a lookout for smuggling and then became a coastguard station until the end of the 1970s. It now belongs to the National Trust and was restored in 2003 as a National Coastwatch Institute lookout.

Leave the tower on its craggy headland and return to the main coast path – you will see a narrow path going left below the tower which drops down to a gate onto the main path, cutting the corner off for you. Descend towards the harbour and when the path forks keep left, taking the option to go down into it rather than keeping on the higher coast path. Savour the area of the harbour, often busy with fishing boats and visitors, and cast your mind back to 2004 when this lovely place made the international news. Devastated by a freak flood a great swathe of this village was laid waste by the power of the torrent. Amazingly no human life was lost. From the harbour wend your way back to the car park.

Looking south west along the coastline

Walk 12

Chapel Porth, St. Agnes & Trevaunance Cove

*A fascinating walk which, in addition to stunning coastal scenery, passes
dramatic mine ruins and climbs to the windy heights of St. Agnes Beacon.
The route also takes in the attractive Churchtown area of St. Agnes. On
a sunny day the turquoise colour of the sea in the coves makes the place
quite magical. There are the usual gradients one would expect with this
kind of terrain.*

Map: OS Explorer 104, Redruth & St. Agnes 1:25 000

Start point: National Trust car park at Chapel Porth. Postcode: TR5 0NS. Grid
ref: SW697494

Directions to start: Chapel Porth is SW of St. Agnes which is on the B3285

Parking: The car park is free to NT members on production of your card

Distance: 6¾ miles / 10.8km

Refreshments: Chapel Porth Beach Café: 01872 552487; The Driftwood Spars,
St. Agnes: 01872 552428; Schooners, St. Agnes: 01872 553149; The Tap House, St.
Agnes: 01872 553095

Toilets: At Chapel Porth and in St. Agnes village

Nearby places to stay: The Aramay, St. Agnes: 01872 553546; Beacon
Cottage Farm Campsite, St. Agnes: 01872 552347; The Driftwood Spars, St. Agnes:
01872 552428; Trevaunance Cottage, St. Agnes: 01872 552419

Nearby places of interest: Blue Hills Tin Streams: 01872 553341

Possible birds include: Blackbird, carrion crow, chiffchaff, feral pigeon, fulmar,
gulls of various hues, house sparrow, jackdaw, linnet, meadow pipit, robin, skylark,
starling, woodpigeon, wren

Authors' tip: Lunch in Schooners is not a bad idea as when conditions are
right you can sit and watch the surfers out in the bay

**Note: Be aware: part of this route is across open moorland, so a map
and compass are needed – and clear weather conditions**

Leave the car park up the road you drove down and a short way
along on the left hand side you will see a sign pointing you up
steps to the coast path and Wheal Coates ½ mile, Trevaunance
Cove 3 miles. Within a couple of hundred metres the path forks
with the left option leading towards a distinctive rocky
promontory. This left fork is what you need and once up on the
rocks you have a fabulous view back down into the bay.

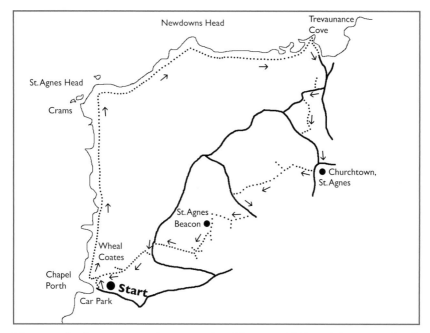

You reach the spectacular mine buildings of Wheal Coates which was in operation during the 19thC and is now owned by the National Trust. From time to time along this route you will see metal structures looking rather like large, conical spiders' webs. These shield old mine shafts so don't poke about!

Continue on the heather-flanked coast path until you reach St. Agnes Head, the coast path swinging right to round the headland. This is about 1½ miles from the start. You will see the little white lookout of the National Coastwatch Institution here and a car park behind the headland. The island you can see is Bawden Rocks, also known as Man and his Man. The route is well-signed with yellow arrows and the coast path acorn marker. Follow the path below the lookout and you will reach the headland of Newdowns.

Keep on the path towards Trevaunance Cove, passing an old, overgrown quarry down on your right. As you approach the cove the views towards it are excellent, look out for sea caves and wonderful rock formations at sea level. Ignore any options to head inland until the path descends down rough-hewn steps towards the cove. Just off these steps is a short path to the right which leads you a few metres to a view over a remarkable stone arch, part of mine ruins. It's worth keeping your eyes open for this spectacular, fern-rich grotto (watch your step on the edges) but if you miss it don't worry, you'll still find the cove.

At the bottom of the steps walk along the path into the cove with its ruined harbour and, thankfully, surviving amenities. The path joins a tarmac drive between buildings and passes some lovely houses and gardens. This drive meets the road through the village, you will see a car park on the left and public loos just over the road. Unless you are exploring / refuelling, the route turns right along the road for about 50m then right again opposite The Driftwood Spars inn.

Approaching Wheal Coates

Sea caves on approach to Trevaunance Cove

This lane climbs past houses. Ignore the footpath on the right and about 300m up from The Driftwood Spars, at a right bend, you will find a footpath on the left signposted for the village. Take this, going up steps, and follow the path beyond to a concrete drive. Cross this and continue up the steps opposite. These lead to a right hand path with a bench and more steps upwards – keep going up the steps.

At the top of the steps a clear path leads ahead, passing an ivy-clad wall on your right before ascending a few more steps. Beyond here the path winds up through a lightly wooded area until it emerges by houses – Roughwood Cottage is on your left with its huge ruined mine by the gate, a garden ornament extraordinaire. Continue ahead, this is Wheal Friendly Lane, passing houses and gardens until you reach the road. There is a Catholic church on your left, turn left and walk along this residential road until you reach the pretty area of Churchtown, the church is in front of you.

Turn right here, passing St. Agnes Hotel on your right. About 30m beyond on the right, set into a terrace of attractive shops, you will find the entrance to a passageway, on the wall of which is a public footpath sign indicating that this is the way to the Beacon and Higher Bal. Take this, passing cottages and climbing to emerge at a residential road. Go straight across here on the footpath signed opposite. You will soon pass a playground on your left and after that the old Churchtown Pump.

The path leads to a stone stile straight ahead, signed for the Beacon. Take this, ignoring the right turn for Higher Bal, and keep ahead through the field, the boundary on your right. Half way through the field the path becomes hedged on both sides then re-emerges and enters another field. Keep on in the same direction until you reach another stile beyond which go straight ahead – you will see a mine chimney over to your right with the sea beyond it. You are heading towards houses. At the far side of this field cross another stone stile. Look behind at this point. The panorama is vast: distant wind farms, patchwork fields, mighty sea cliffs. After the stile keep ahead in the same line and the next stile leads onto a lane.

Ignore the footpath opposite and turn left here, passing houses until, in 300m, you reach a broad bridleway on your right signed for the Beacon. Take this. When the track bears right you will see three possible choices: ahead, right with the main track and even more right. Keep on the main track which is, in effect, the middle option. Climb on upwards, the superb coastal views easing the strain a little, until you reach a gate ahead and one on the left. Pass through the one straight ahead and beyond it take the path to the left, still climbing towards a high point. A trig point comes into view. Head for it. It can be phenomenally windy here – hang onto your contact lenses. Beyond the trig head downhill in the same direction as before (roughly south) on the well-trodden path. Houses are well below you and to your right you can see a caravan

The Harbour

The Tonkin family, lords of the manor of Trevaunance, monopolised the mining wealth of this area. With a view to opening up trade from Ireland and Wales they set about constructing a harbour at Trevaunance Cove. The first attempt in 1632 was destroyed before completion in the winter gales whilst a second, in  1684, met a similar fate. A third harbour, in 1699, was designed by Henry Winstanley, who found fame for the construction of Eddystone Lighthouse the previous year. More professionally built than its predecessors, this one managed to last for six years before a storm again destroyed it. In 1709 another harbour was built in a similar style to the third, but this was ultimately washed away in 1730. By now the Tonkin family were hopelessly in debt and their estate had to be relinquished. In 1793 an act of parliament was passed allowing for a fifth harbour to be built. Within the act was a stipulation that work had to be completed within seven years. With the impetus of a copper mining boom, construction began and a new harbour was completed in 1798 by the St. Agnes Harbour Co. It saw plenty of use for over 100 years with its major export being copper to Wales. Materials imported here were lime, slate, wine and, most importantly, coal from South Wales for the smelters at the mines. In 1802, the harbour enabled the development of a pilchard fishing industry, reaching its peak in 1829/30 before going into decline. St. Agnes remained a busy port until the collapse of this fifth and final harbour during the storms of 1915/16. Several of the granite blocks remain clearly visible at the foot of the cliffs on the left hand side of the beach.

site with old mine buildings beyond on the coast. The caravan site is where you are heading, which is worth bearing in mind through the next bit!

Keep your eyes well peeled now, ignoring any individual paths off until, about 300m from the trig point, you reach a small crossing path (grid ref SW709499) at which you keep straight on for another 10m to a fork in the path. Go right at the fork, you are now heading towards the coast. Keep ahead now, ignoring any forks, until you soon reach a stone-stepped stile (grid ref SW708499). Cross this and walk through the next field with the boundary on your right. Reassuring yellow arrows direct you. When the boundary ends keep going as before to the end of the field. There is a huge granite stone to your left and a gate with a footpath fingerpost. Go through the gate and continue through the yard beyond in the direction indicated by the post. Pass the buildings of Beacon Cottage Farm Campsite until you reach the lane. Turn left.

Go along the lane for 100m until, on your right, you find the National Trust car park for Wheal Coates. Here you'll find the footpath back to Chapel Porth. Follow this, rounding the car park on your left, and at the end of the car park you find a crossing path. Keep straight ahead here and the path starts to drop down towards the cove at Chapel Porth. You will see crossing paths but keep heading down towards the sea, your car and tea.

Trevaunance Cove